DISCARD

D1361101

ALTA COMMUNITY LIBRARY
1009 MAIN STREET
ALTA. IOWA 51002

14.50 Amer. Kids Preview 11-18-05 SP

After-school
FUN

Music Lessons

by JoAnn Early Macken

Reading consultant: Susan Nations, M.Ed., author/literacy coach/consultant

WR WEEKLY READER
EARLY LEARNING LIBRARY

Please visit our web site at: **www.earlyliteracy.cc**
For a free color catalog describing Weekly Reader® Early Learning Library's list
of high-quality books, call 1-877-445-5824 (USA) or 1-800-387-3178 (Canada).
Weekly Reader® Early Learning Library's fax: (414) 336-0164.

Library of Congress Cataloging-in-Publication Data

Macken, JoAnn Early, 1953-
　　Music lessons / by JoAnn Early Macken.
　　　　p. cm. — (After-school fun)
　　Includes bibliographical references and index.
　　ISBN 0-8368-4515-3 (lib. bdg.)
　　ISBN 0-8368-4522-6 (softcover)
　　1. Instrumental music—Performance—Juvenile literature.
　　2. Instrumental music—Instruction and study—Juvenile literature.
　　I. Title.
　　ML460.M26　　2005
　　784.193'071—dc22　　　　　　　　　　　　　　　2004061177

This edition first published in 2005 by
Weekly Reader® Early Learning Library
330 West Olive Street, Suite 100
Milwaukee, WI 53212 USA

Copyright © 2005 by Weekly Reader® Early Learning Library

Photographer: Gregg Andersen
Picture research: Diane Laska-Swanke
Art direction and page layout: Tammy West

All rights reserved. No part of this book may be reproduced, stored in a retrieval system,
or transmitted in any form or by any means, electronic, mechanical, photocopying,
recording, or otherwise, without the prior written permission of the copyright holder.

Printed in the United States of America

1 2 3 4 5 6 7 8 9 09 08 07 06 05

Note to Educators and Parents

Reading is such an exciting adventure for young children! They are beginning to integrate their oral language skills with written language. To encourage children along the path to early literacy, books must be colorful, engaging, and interesting; they should invite the young reader to explore both the print and the pictures.

After-School Fun is a new series designed to help children read about the kinds of activities they enjoy in their free time. In each book, young readers learn about a different artistic endeavor, physical activity, or learning experience.

Each book is specially designed to support the young reader in the reading process. The familiar topics are appealing to young children and invite them to read — and reread — again and again. The full-color photographs and enhanced text further support the student during the reading process.

In addition to serving as wonderful picture books in schools, libraries, homes, and other places where children learn to love reading, these books are specifically intended to be read within an instructional guided reading group. This small group setting allows beginning readers to work with a fluent adult model as they make meaning from the text. After children develop fluency with the text and content, the book can be read independently. Children and adults alike will find these books supportive, engaging, and fun!

— Susan Nations, M.Ed., author, literacy coach,
and consultant in literacy development

After school, I go to my piano lesson. My teacher shows me how to place my hands on the keys. I learn how to play a chord.

I learn how to play scales. A **scale** is a series of notes. My fingers move up and down the keyboard. I play high notes and low notes.

I am learning how to read music. I find the notes on the staff. I play the keys on the piano. I can play a song!

My friend is learning
to play the violin. She
holds it under her chin.
She plays the violin
with a bow.

Her fingers move up and down the neck of the violin. She presses on the strings to change the notes she plays.

She plays in a group
called a **string quartet**.
The quartet has four
members. Two play
the violin. One plays
the viola. One plays
the cello.

My cousin plays the saxophone. She blows through a mouthpiece. She presses buttons, or **keys**, to play notes.

She plays in the band at her school. The band meets every day to practice.

Someday, I may join a band or an orchestra. I will play my favorite music. What kind of music do you like?

Glossary

bow — a wooden rod with horsehairs stretched from end to end that is used to play stringed instruments

chord — a group of notes that are played or sung at the same time

note — a symbol for a musical tone

scale — a series of notes played or sung up and down in order of pitch

staff — a set of five lines on which musical notes are written. A note placed on each line or space stands for a different pitch.

For More Information

Books

Meet the Marching Smithereens. Ann Hayes (Harcourt Brace)

Musical Instruments from A to Z. Bobbie Kalman (Crabtree)

Sound and Music. David Evans and Claudette Williams (Dorling Kindersley)

The Story of the Incredible Orchestra: An Introduction to Musical Instruments and the Symphony Orchestra. Bruce Koscielniak (Houghton Mifflin)

Web Sites

The Science of Music from Exploratorium
www.exploratorium.edu/music/
Compose music, mix sounds, build rhythms

ALTA COMMUNITY LIBRARY
1009 MAIN STREET
ALTA, IOWA 51002

Index

About the Author

JoAnn Early Macken is the author of two rhyming picture books, *Sing-Along Song* and *Cats on Judy*, and six other series of nonfiction books for beginning readers. Her poems have appeared in several children's magazines. A graduate of the M.F.A. in Writing for Children and Young Adults program at Vermont College, she lives in Wisconsin with her husband and their two sons. Visit her Web site at www.joannmacken.com.

DISCARD

DISCARD